WHAT CAME FIRST

THE CHICKEN OR THE EGG?

REAL COURCHESNE

Printed in the United States of America.

Library of Congress Control Number: 2022948290

ISBN	Paperback	978-1-68536-916-3
	eBook	978-1-68536-918-7

Westwood Books Publishing LLC
Atlanta Financial Center
3343 Peachtree Rd NE Ste 145-725
Atlanta, GA 30326

www.westwoodbookspublishing.com

The chicken or the egg?

Our race is currently engaged on the road to another planet in the universe.

The universe is infinite in all directions. it never had a beginning, and will never end.

TABLE OF CONTENTS

INTRODUCTION

This book is independent and is bound to no association with any religion or political party. This entirely personal approach allows me to talk about things that fascinate me. My goal is to denounce fake science, which rarely cares about the consequences of the information it spreads and largely escapes our understanding.

Religious fanaticism is still very palpable in the world today. This book draws our attention to some false religious prophets, as well as scientists who still today, teach anything no matter what.

This book examines some scientific teachings or words of God accepted as truth by many people and some or academic circles.

This book questions the origin of religions as the fundamental value of modern science: the Law of the Big Bang, for example.

This book provides information voluntarily hidden by some religious and scientific leaders who do not reveal all the facts.

Pertaining to my own beliefs, I have to say that we are negligent concerning our presumptions. Education is not everything, we need *quality education*. It is perilous to teach anything, especially to young children, as it becomes very difficult, often impossible to forget false precepts received in our childhood. On the other hand, being educated is not a guarantee. We are always at the mercy of potential errors of judgement or belief. Education is a never-ending process of inquiry in which openness is the fundamental value. Then, I expose some simple personal analyses of the spokesmen of God or science.

I consider myself to be open to the progress of science and fundamentally religious, maybe because of my roots. At twenty, I am interested in many religions as the Catholic tradition. During my 15 years of study of several Christian Doctrines and the beliefs of the Jehovah's witnesses, without joining their ranks, I wondered where some of them received there in formations.

At the age of thirty-seven, I became a member of the Church of Jesus of Latter-day Saints (Mormons) for the next seven years. Still, from a very young age, my religious delight is tainted by disappointments generated by some too-obvious converses.

CHAPTER 1

The chicken or the egg?

"What came first: the chicken or the egg?"

The question has been haunting humanity since the dawn of time. The paradox of the egg and the chicken is one of the oldest and most prevalent examples of the vicious circles that provokes the belief in the creation of the universe from nothing.

What came first: the chicken or the egg?

If the response is *"It's the egg,"* ask, *"But who laid this egg?"*

If another response is *"The chicken,"* ask, *"But this hen came out from an egg, right?"* It takes an egg, a hen, and the sperm of a rooster to fertilize the egg; which of the three entities was created first if one cannot exist without the other?

It is imperative to resolve this paradox. The Enigma is repeated in many other creatures *(animal, vegetal, earthly celestial).*

While we look at the origins of a tree, one is asked the following question: *"What came first? The tree or his seed?*

If the response is, *"It's the tree,"* you ask, *"Does not the tree came from the seed that fell from another tree, which was fertilized by the pollen of another tree?"*

CHAPTER 2

The formation of a star

The stars are like us: they are born, they live, and die.

It is similar for all planets that fill the universe. Planets are formed from dust and clumps of gas floating in the universe.

The formation of the *Solar System* begins billions of years before with the *gravitational collapse* of a small part of a giant *molecular cloud*. Most of the collapsing mass collected in the center, formed the *Sun*. At the same time, the rest flattened into a *protoplanetary disk* out of which the *planets, moons, asteroids,* and other *small Solar System bodies* formed.

We know that not all stars are born in massive molecular clouds. Some are born among the less massive, and are formed from smaller molecular clouds. During the contraction, the cloud breaks up. Fragments of mass greater than a few solar masses condense in turn and will form stars.

Those planets need molecular clouds to be born, which are produced by the gas and the particles released by smouldering or exploding planets and galaxies; this principle is eternal because other planets had to be born, live for some time and die before a molecular cloud is formed, and then the creation of a new world is possible.

A planet could never be born if no other existed before it. Stars and galaxies form at the center of molecular clouds. *Molecular clouds* are made up of gas and debris of planets and stars.

Some scientists believe that our solar system was formed when a cloud of gas and dust in space was disturbed, maybe by the explosion of a nearby star called a *supernova*.

This explosion sent shockwaves into space, squeezing the cloud of gas and dust. Gravity drew the gas and dust together, producing a solar system, compressing the cloud and causing it to collapse. It started to spin faster and began to collapse. The cloud eventually became hotter and denser in the center, surrounded by a disk of gas and dust that was heated in the core but cold at the edges. As the disk got thinner and thinner, particles began to stick together and form clumps. Some clumps got bigger, as particles and small clumps stuck to them, eventually forming *planets or moons*;

Near the center of the cloud, where planets like *Earth* formed, only rocky material could stand the great heat. The icy matter settled in the meantime disk's outer region along with rocky material, where giant planets like *Jupiter* formed. As the cloud continued to fall in, the center eventually got so hot that it became a star, our Sun.

If some Bible translators did not teach us to be obsessed with certain things, preaching that the world came from nothing would mean that the egg, the chicken, and everything else on Earth and in the universe has always been there.

CHAPTER 3

What is the universe?

Imagine the universe as something huge, bigger than anything we know, even bigger than you can imagine! Researchers are studying this topic daily, struggling to understand what the universe looks like. The universe contains planets, stars, galaxies, quasars, black holes, comets, particles, gas, dust that travel randomly in space, and perhaps even some aliens. But in reality, no one understands exactly what it looks like. At the time of the explosion, some of the elements came from the stars. As far as looking into the world with the largest telescopes, we see galaxies, regardless of the direction we look at.

Astronomers have discovered galaxies more than 10 billion light-years and considering that there are others still farther. Is there a limit? And is the universe eternal? did it have a beginning? Surely, nobody can tell today! We can only make theories.

Seemingly, scientists agree that our solar system is the result of contraction, due to its mass, a dense interstellar molecular cloud made of gas, hydrogen, helium, and grains of dust covered with water ice.

A disc of material formed, slowly turning on itself on the outskirts, quickly to the Center. At the disc's heart, the matter is more compressed by the movement. As the temperature increases, nuclear fusion reactions would eventually occur. This heart would then have to reach a phenomenal energy, giving birth to our Sun.

The rest of the cloud would have continued to gravitate around this new star, the most volatile compounds rejected in the periphery due to the high temperature. In this Nebula, dust would be gradually assembled, forming grains that would be joined by boulders, which is substantially in would have slowly given birth to the nine planets of our solar system, meteorites and their satellites.

Images of collisions between several galaxies taken by Hubble show that galaxies are rarely isolated. They belong to more or less big groups, from a few galaxies (called groups) to thousands of galaxies (called clusters). These clusters are grouped in *Superclusters* that are attracted between them. A supercluster is a long bar of 300 to 900 million light-years long and 100 to 150 light-years large. For example, the *"great wall"* spans 500 million light years.

Giant elliptical galaxies are often at the center of a cluster. These galaxies are usually the result of two galaxies running into each other or a galaxy that pulls in its neighbors. The further away from the center, the more spiral galaxies there are.

Ancient people thought that the stars were always in the same place in the sky. Now, astronomers know that the universe is so big that its edges are unknown.

The *Theory of Stationary State*, a cosmological model proposed in the late 1940s by Fred Hoyle, Thomas Gold, and Hermann Bondi, assuming that the universe is eternal and immutable, would be good.

ISO, the space observatory in the infrared, directed by the European Space Agency and operated with the participation of NASA, helped a team of American astronomers discover a large concentration of water vapor in a cloud of interstellar gas close to the nebula of Orion. ISO found water vapor in many parts of the universe, from the outer planets of the solar system to distant galaxies. However, the concentration reached this time is 20 times greater than previously observed in other interstellar gas clouds.

The matter consists of particles called *atoms*. Planets, air, water, stones, living things, and all-natural bodies are formed from atoms or assemblies of atoms (molecules). The atoms of an element are all identical, but they differ from one element to another. Minerals are different from plants. For example, gold is an element that contains only gold atoms, and hydrogen is an element containing only hydrogen atoms. Two or more atoms can bind chemically to form a compound. It is estimated that the size of the atom is of the order of 0.1 nm (0.0000000001 meters).

CHAPTER 4

The Big Bang theory

The Big Bang is a cosmological model used by some scientists to describe the origin and evolution of the universe. It was initially proposed in 1927 by the Catholic Bishop Georges Lemaître, an astronomer and physicist. His theory of the Big Bang explains the beginning to the universe, which many of the creation's religious leaders accepted.

A priest who, throughout his life, will have to fight twice is the first to admit a revolutionary worldview. Then, acknowledge that it is not religious. The very concept of the beginning of the universe triggered a storm of protest. This smells too much of Genesis, especially coming from a priest. Whenever he hears of the primitive Atom, Einstein exclaims: "No, not that, this is too close to the creation already proclaim by his church!" Lemaître says that instead his theory describes a purely natural beginning of the universe, which gave strong support to the Big Bang theory.

But what would lead Lemaître to an excessive intellectual adventure? It is, by his admission, a double vocation who seized him when he was nine years old, and he decided to become a scholar and priest. Until his last breath, he said that it was two different paths towards the truth.

The Big Bang theory claims that every part of the universe grew simultaneously from a tiny point in a total vacuum. But how could these parts produce the beginning of their expansion?

With a mysterious explosion, the universe Springs, releasing a tremendous amount of material and energy, it's the Big Bang. According to those who advocate the Big Bang, there was only a tiny point that exploded during a period dense and hot that would have undergone the universe about 13.7 billion years ago.

But the origin of this tiny point is still unknown to the scientific community.

A question then arises, why do these scientists never talk about the provenance of this tiny point in which all the universes was locked up?

But let's look at the credibility of this theory; The emptiness does not contain anything; Nothing - doesn't have a precise value for the person who owns it because nothing equals nothing. Emptiness is a complete absence of element. If this point, as tiny as it could have been, holding the entire universe had existed in the emptiness as they try to explain, this sort of empty space was not total because of this point!

Try to imagine the immensity of the universe that grew up at the same time, instantly, from a tiny point in total emptiness. This theory belongs to the miracles, a creation by a God!

This explosion would have launched to infinity, everything found in the universe; and would continue to move away from each other. And yet, astronomers have long known that far away from moving away, the milky way, our Galaxy, is on a collision course with the nearby spiral galaxy of Andromeda. A galactic collision is predicted to occur in about 4 billion years between the two largest galaxies, the Andromeda Galaxy and the Milky Way, our galaxy. It is approaching ours at the speed of 500,000 km/h.

To justify the theory of the Big Bang, some scientists suggest that an observer in any Galaxy could see that most of the other galaxies in the universe are moving away from each other. If the galaxies were moving away from each other at a greater speed than they are distant, imagine the distance they would now have reached between each other after 13.7 billion years.

Assuming that billions of galaxies are moving away from each other as they claim, how could this system end its wild race if the universe is not out of the boundary, eternal? What would be the impact as they hit the limit of the universe?

Another paradox is that the universe would have been hot about 13.7 billion years ago, which would have caused this tiny point where the whole universe was concentrated to explode. This is because the universe was still inside the little point before it exploded, so it couldn't have heated up and exploded if it didn't exist.

Furthermore, given that magnetic and electrostatic attraction provides the foundation for the functioning of atoms, planets, and galaxies, the distance of the galaxies would not be an exception to the rule.

I'm astonished to see many scientists proclaiming the Theory of the Big Bang.

The followers of this theory must also admit that this emanates from the same entity as its content! According to the dictionary *Antidote,* the absolute void represents a theoretical environment characterized by a total absence of any physical particle. As I said, it could not cause that period dense and hot that would have known the universe about 13.7 billion years ago to trigger the explosion if the universe was not yet created? How could the universe heat up if it did not exist before the explosion?

The information about the Big Bang is hypothetical because scientists do not have all the information about this period.

CHAPTER 5

The theory of a creation emerging from nothing If we were born under the influence of Catholic, Protestant, or some other religions, chances are we already believe in *a creation out of nothing*. Why do they teach that God would create the universe from nothing when (the Bible) explains that there was a formless and invalid Earth before the creation started? Darkness was upon the face of the deep. The Spirit of God moved upon the face of the waters.

To believe that God created the heaven and the Earth from nothing, we must add it ourselves; the Bible never mentioned it.

"Having always existed"

Is the sentence: *"Having always existed"* and *"If I was creating a world"* beyond our understanding?

Suppose God has eternally existed, as we are taught by most religions, but not the universe. What was God doing during the billions of years before creating the universe?

Why did God as smart as described, who never had a beginning, remain useless? However, after a period of time, He who made billions of years, as small as a drop of water in the ocean, suddenly decides to create the universe.

No matter when he created the universe, the time between having being forever and the date He created the world is innumerable, beyond description. The theory of a God who existed eternally, but not the universe, seems very unconvincing to me.

CHAPTER 6

Religions

Religion takes an important role in the culture of human societies.

Religions and beliefs in God are often the basis for significant conflict, even the source of world wars.

It seems that we humans, are really slow to understand. For example, the Catholic Church, encouraged many Crusades (1st Crusade: 1098-1099; 3rd Crusade: 1189-1192) against Muslims. During the *Inquisition,* where ten thousand of people were burned alive and millions of "infidels" were killed just to make us understand that Catholicism is a *religion of love*.

1.57 billion Faithful Muslims from Iraq, Afghanistan and other countries, are available today for martyrdom by wrapping themselves in a belt of bombs and explode amid the biggest crowds of infidels (non-Muslim) to prove to the world that Islam is the most acceptable religion and that it must dominate the Earth.

The utility of religions

What has the value of collaboration with other religions been in global history, excluding the value of internal love among members?

Have they brought peace in the world? Have they helped in the development of Science in some way? Have they improved the love between nations in the world? Have they brought the truth concerning our world's creation or our origin? Unfortunately, the answer is No.

If we continue to support them, what benefit are there left for our descendants?

Three major religions today are operated by dictators who are passionate about powers, each claiming to be the only-one having the truth; *Judaism, Christianity and Islam,* which all explicitly refer to the same Patriarch, Abraham.

Christians believe in the same God as Jews and Muslims, but they have their particularity. Each religion has grown in a particular environment, with its culture and history; each one has a founder whose revelations are received as *divine* and *decisive.*

Thus, in the affirmation of the existence of God, the Jews stated that it is *Moses* who gave the Torah and revealed the way of living the faith in God. Muslims say it's *Mohammed* who gave the Koran and showed the way of living in the faith in God. Christians make clear that it is *Jesus of*

Nazareth who revealed God and the way of living in the faith in God through his life and death.

The perception of religious faith is similar everywhere regardless if they are Muslim, Christian, Jewish or Buddhist. Defaming a religion inevitably hurt his faithful members. Karl Marx, a philosopher and historian, was quite accurate declaring that *"religion is the opium of the people."*

All the time, religion was and still is the most important cause for wars. From Martin Luther to Bin Laden, millions and millions of people died for God.

A monk displayed on the door of the Church of Wittenberg (Saxony) 95 on October 31, 1517, where he denounced the scandals in the Church of his time. Unsuspectingly, Martin Luther lays the foundations for *Protestantism*, a new kind of Christianity.

Martin Luther, 34 years old, questions the access to eternal life. His reflections led him to denounce the hierarchy Catholic of his time, mocking the Gospel.

The first were scandals denounced by Luther in his *95 theses*.

In 1517, Luther penned a document attacking the Catholic Church's corrupt practice of selling *"indulgences"* or the *abuse of indulgences*. It's the alms that clergy harvest against the promise of relief from the penalties that await sinners in purgatory, in the antechamber of heaven.

Despite the fact that indulgences may be obtained through different sacrifices, the sacrifice of money is very well seen by the Catholic Church. In other words, liberation from sin is determined by the purchasing power of indulgences; *money is an antidote* against the penalties caused by sin that await sinners in purgatory.

Considering that Christians need no intermediate to love God, Martin Luther opposes Rome that he presents as their *'red prostitute of Babylon.'*

Meanwhile, the Catholic Church's practice of granting *"indulgences"* to provide absolution to sinners became increasingly corrupt. *Indulgence-selling* had been banned in Germany, but the practice continued unabated. In 1517, a friar named Johann Tetzel began to sell indulgences in Germany to raise funds to renovate St. Peter's Basilica in Rome.

Committed to the idea that salvation could be reached through faith and by divine grace only, Luther vigorously objected to the corrupt practice of selling indulgences.

Acting on this belief, he wrote the *"Disputation on the Power and Efficacy of Indulgences,"* also known as *"The 95 Theses,"* a list of questions and propositions for debate. Popular legend has it that on October 31, 1517, Luther defiantly nailed a copy of his 95 Theses to the door of the Wittenberg Castle church.

Threatened by the imperial armies, Protestants formed the *Schmalkaldic League* and called to their aid the great rival of Charles Quint, the King of France François 1st, a Catholic worthy of admiration.

As a result, from 1561 to 1598, he followed a succession of massacres and true eight *'wars'* in total between the two camps. Nearly two million victims, with additional famines, diseases, and food shortages than actual wars say.

Since the existence of the first religion (Egypt, India, or other) until today, how many human beings have been killed in the name of God by religions recognized as a way to worship God?

Examples are the hate between Muslims-Jews Arabs and the current conflict of interest between the Taliban against the U.S., England, and Canada.

Even celebrities are doing it today: Madonna, Britney Spears, and Tom Cruise belong to religion like *"Scientology."*

It is disturbing to imagine those children and all those who have these people as models or idols joined or are joining in a few years.

Mel Gibson, sparked controversy between Jews and Christians in 2004 through his film *The Passion of Christ.*

Religious terrorism in New York and Washington

The first attack on the World Trade Center in 1993 by Islamic fundamentalists was the massacre of 30 Muslim worshippers at the tomb of the Patriarchs by a Jewish extremist in 1994.

September 11, 2001: *BIN LADEN and BUSH acted in the name of God!*

A few hours after the terrorist attacks of September 11 at the World Trade Center and the Pentagon, the Bush Administration concluded, without evidence in support, that Osama Bin Laden and his organization, Al-Qaeda, were the most likely suspects. Secretary of State Colin Powell called these attacks in Washington and New York of *"declarations of war,"* which George Bush confirmed in his speech to the Nation the same evening by saying it won't make any distinction between the terrorists who committed these acts and those who supported them

On October 8, 2001, the world saw a video of Osama Bin Laden and heard his statement: *"the Holy war against the Jews and the Christians started…"* Allah has blessed a group of leading Muslim to destroy America. Allah blesses them and gives them a place in heaven.

Osama Bin Laden understood religion's importance in motivating people to give their lives and to make themselves reach their goals. On behalf of Saddam Hussein, he appealed to God repeatedly against an *"evil enemy."*

The attack of terrorists on the United States is still incomprehensible. Everything so far is simply inconceivable. Osama Bin Laden and his terrorist organization dared to destroy the World Trade Center in New York. In 105 minutes, the proud skyscrapers were reduced in debris and ash. Thousands of people died in this hell.

However, the main objective of terrorists was to miss the residence of USA's president, the White House. Only a few metres away, a plane rushed into the leading Pentagon of hundreds of military and civilian employees in death. The practice of terror in various countries is undoubtedly known. Still, the attack against the United States gave a new dimension to *holy war or jihad.*

The new Pope declares war on those who resist against Jewish occupation in Palestine to defend Israel! Benedict appealed to a text of the fourteenth century to *demonstrate* that Christianity is more apt than Islam to cohabit with the reason. Still, the Muslim world is asking for an apology from the Catholic Church.

We were taught in school that the nine Crusades, which lasted 179 years and claimed millions of lives, were a holy war. Nothing more awful existed than the *Catholic Inquisition!*

Then, we learned that for 36 years, the *Calvinist Protestants* demanding recognition of their cult made a deadly war against their Catholic opponents, who treated them as sinful. Then came the *holy inquisition*, which for almost four centuries, confiscated, imprisoned, tortured, and executed all whom the ecclesiastical judges condemned as heretics at stake.

The idea of an afterlife with God is reassuring, while we have certain apprehensions about death. Almost all religions collide with this genuine question: *what is there after death?* Man is the only rational or living creature aware and can anticipate his death. He also knows that he cannot escape it no matter what.

Many religions that seem desirable, useful, and even necessary for the proper functioning of society are often very dangerous and even harmful because of their intolerance towards other religions or organizations.

Although I firmly believe that a force exists in the universe, called God. However, I agree with Freud, the Father of Psychoanalysis.

According to Freud, *Religion* is an obstacle to the intellectual development of mankind. It is a disease of a psychic nature. *Thinking is forbidden* because it prevents us from finding rational explanations for the questions we ask ourselves.

It would therefore prevent us from being logical. According to Freud, it keeps men *infantilism*, a situation that artificially prolongs a natural state. It maintains a biological and psychological immaturity.

We saw that it was impossible that a chicken could have existed unless there was an egg and a rooster who produced the sperm to fertilize it. We noticed that a tree could not be created by only the seed planted by another unless it is fertilized by *the pollen of another tree.* We also saw that to be born, planets need molecular clouds, produced by the gas and the particles that release the planets and galaxies in smouldering or exploding in a collision with other planets. This principle turns out to be eternal, because, other planets had to be born and die before a molecular cloud formed, and the creation of a new planet is possible.

CHAPTER 7

Albert Einstein

Albert Einstein was born on March 14, 1879, in Ulm, Württemberg, and died on April 18, 1955, in Princeton, New Jersey. He was a physicist and was successively German, then became stateless (1896), then became a Swiss (1901), and finally became under dual citizenship Helvético-Américains (1940).

He received the Nobel Prize for Physics in 1921 for explaining the *photoelectric effect*. He is considered today as one of the greatest scientists in history, and his fame reached far beyond the scientific community. The Ttheory of Relativity was developed by Albert Einstein in the early 20th century. In 1905, he presented his article on the electrodynamics of moving bodies, published in the German scientific journal Annalen der Physik (Annals of Physics). Subsequently presents the General Relativity (1915), which extends the previous.

Albert Einstein's theory, which appears today much less justified, is that *the universe is static* and *does not change with time*, so *it is stable and eternal*. His theory is clearly contradictory to that of creation preached by the Churches.

In 1917, Einstein initiated modern cosmology by postulating, based on general relativity, a homogeneous, static, spatially curved universe. He established the *Cosmological Constant* to prevent gravitational contraction. In 1922 Alexander Friedman showed that Albert Einstein's fundamental equations also allow dynamic worlds. Additionally, Georges Lemaître, backed by his observational evidence, concluded that *our universe was expanding* in 1927. Einstein rejected Friedman's as well as Lemaitre's findings.

However, Einstein retracted his former Static Model in favour of a dynamic solution in 1931 *the universe is static, does not evolve with time,* so stable and eternal, and so obviously contradicts the Doctrine of Creation by the Catholic Church and some of our scientists. Aristotle denies any theory of evolution, which had already been made by Democritus, a Greek philosopher. He also declared the eternal existence of *genus or species.*

Lemaître was eclipsed by several textbooks proclaiming Hubble as the discoverer of the *expanding universe.* However, Hubble himself never believed such a theory.

Suddenly, in 2011, a burst of accusations has flared up against Hubble, from the suspicion that censorship was exerted either on Lemaître by the editor of the M.N.R.A.S. or on the editor by Hubble himself, fear based on the *complex personality* of Hubble, who strongly desired to be credited with the Hubble constant.

The Big Bang theory is based on the work of Monsignor Georges Lemaitre, a Belgian Catholic Canon, astronomer, and physicist, who used his *Primitive Atom Theory* to explain the creation of the universe. Based on his calculations, the Belgian astronomer attempted to demonstrate that the universe had a beginning and was, in fact, growing constantly. Indeed, something triggered this expansion. He then established that radiation levels could be used as a measure of the consequence of this *something*.

In 1927, independent from the work of Alexander Friedman, Georges Lemaître, published an article in the annals of the scientific society of Brussels called *a homogeneous universe of constant mass and RADIUS croissant2*, establishing that the universe is expanding, putting an end to Albert Einstein's limited and general *Theory of Relativity*.

Theoretical analyses of these two scientists were mostly uninteresting. They likely would have been forgotten if new experimental considerations hadn't disturbed the scientific community in 1929. This year, the American astronomer Edwin Hubble, working for the Wilson of Mount California Observatory, made an astronomical discovery. Using his enormous telescope, he observed the stars. He determined that the Albert Einstein's initial idea was that redshirt of light was precisely proportional to the distance between the stars and Earth. This revelation disturbed the conceptual foundation of the then-prevailing concept of the *perpetual universe in* force until then.

Edwin Hubble's discovery that the universe is expanding was accepted. Finally, it was proven that the Big Bang was a cataclysmic event. This forced the scientists to abandon the notion of an infinite and eternal universe.

Extracts from a letter written by Albert Einstein to the philosopher Eric Gutkind on January 3, 1954, provide the official refutation to all those who claim that he was a believer.

Unsurprisingly, the letter was bought at auction in May 2008 for £170,000.

Nothing was done to enhance its connection with Catholic astronomers and physicists. A year before his death, he said that the concept of God was born of human weakness and called the Bible *"really childish."*

Princeton, 3. 1. 1954

Dear Mr Gutkind,

Inspired by Brower's repeated suggestion, I read a great deal in your book, and thank you very much for lending it to me. What struck me was this: with regard to the factual attitude to life and to the human community we have a great deal in common. Your personal ideal with its striving for freedom from ego-oriented desires, for making life beautiful and noble, with an emphasis on the purely human element. This unites us as having an "un-American attitude."

Still, without Brower's suggestion I would never have gotten myself to engage intensively with your book because it is written in a language inaccessible to me. The word God is for me nothing more than the expression and product of human weakness, the Bible a collection of honorable, but still purely primitive, legends which are nevertheless pretty childish. No interpretation, no matter how subtle, can change this for me. For me the Jewish religion like all other religions is an incarnation of the most childish superstition. And the Jewish people to whom I gladly belong and whose thinking I have a deep affinity for, have no different quality for me than all other people. As far as my experience goes, they are also no better than other human groups, although they are protected from the worst cancers by a lack of power. Otherwise I cannot see anything "chosen" about them.

In general I find it painful that you claim a privileged position and try to defend it by two walls of pride, an external one as a man and an internal one as a Jew. As a man you claim, so to speak, a dispensation from causality otherwise accepted, as a Jew the privilege of monotheism. But a limited causality is no longer a causality at all, as our wonderful Spinoza recognized with all incision, probably as the first one. And the animistic interpretations of the religions of nature are in principle not annulled by monopolization. With such walls we can only attain a certain self-deception, but our moral efforts are not furthered by it on the contrary.

Now that I have quite openly stated our differences in intellectual convictions it is still clear to me that we are quite close to each other in essential things, ; in our evaluations of human behavior. What separates us are only intellectual "props" and "rationalization" in Freud's language. Therefore I think that we would understand each other quite well if we talked about concrete things.

With friendly thanks and best wishes,

Yours,

A. Einstein

No wonder Lemaître and all the religious power leading the education and a large part of the governments in the world, made sure that Albert Einstein's theory, contradicting the creation preached by the Catholic Religion, be vanished from the shelf of our institutions.

Most of the great scientists of the past believed in God and took the Bible seriously. For example, the *Institute of Creation Research* (USA), lists 31 such scientists together with the scientific disciplines they helped to establish. They include Kepler (astronomy), Pascal (hydrostatics), Boyle (chemistry), Newton (calculus), Linnaeus (systematic biology), Faraday (electromagnetics), Cuvier (comparative anatomy), Kelvin (thermodynamics), Lister (antiseptic surgery), Mendel (genetics), and many other equally famous names.

Christian Europe was the birthplace of experiential Science three centuries before the rise of Darwinism. It did so precisely because of the almost universal belief in a Creator God.

Why did the *Founding Fathers of Modern Science* believe in a God who created the universe?

For one simple reason: *the natural world exhibits all the characteristics of "Intelligent Design."*

This powerful evidence for the existence of an Intelligent Designer who created the universe has certainly been the view of most of the great philosophers and thinkers of the past, like Socrates, Plato, Aristotle, Cicero, Aquinas, Bacon, and Newton, etc. They recognized the credibility of God's existence – as did Immanuel Kant (18th century), despite his rejection of all the traditional arguments for God's existence except the moral one.

Like many other religious theories, the Catholic Church teaches that God Himself was never created. He existed in the past, and will continue to exist eternally in the future.

Is it so difficult to imagine that the universe could also be eternal if God is eternal?

CHAPTER 8

Space travelling

The concept of space travel, to the Moon, or to another planet is very old.

The concept of sending a man into space was evoked by philosophers and novelists hundreds of years before it became physically feasible.

In 1882, Jules Verne walked on the Moon in imagination.

Let's travel back to 1865 and 1870 to understand that Jules Verne authored his novel about a voyage to and around the moon in 1865 and 1870. Jules Verne Albert Einstein's initial idea was born February 8, 1828, in Nantes

France, and died on March 24, 1905, in Amiens France. He French whose majority of works are science fiction adventure novels. It is structured on assumptions to determine what might have been and what might happen in the future!

Almost all the "Extraordinaire Voyages" written by Jules Verne refer to astronomy. In some of them, astronomy is even the leading subject. Jules Verne was basically not learned in science. His knowledge of astronomy came from popular publications and discussions with specialists among his friends or his family.

With his trip to the Moon (1865) and around the Moon (1870), Jules Verne made a significant contribution to this technology by introducing *scientific realism* for the first time. Jules Verne has revolutionized our way of thought. This informs us on how astronomy was understood by an *"honnête homme"* in the late 19th century.

Additionally, we heard about the Wright brothers, two prominent American Aviation pioneers who conducted the first controlled flight on December 17, 1903, at Kitty Hawk, North Carolina. We achieved the first controlled flights and motors in the history of aviation.

One of Jules Verne's novels: *from the Earth to the Moon,* describes how a Barbican shell launched from a cannon created by engineer Barbican is currently on its way to the Moon. The three passengers who took place are going to be witnesses of extraordinary events: *the discovery of weightlessness that makes them float inside their gunshot; the encounter with an asteroid that alters their path;* and *finally, the overview of the moon.* Soon, we'll ask an agonizing question: *will they be able to land on the Moon?* Jules Verne's story about a journey to the moon gives off the scent of the supernatural.

Today, we're talking about extraterrestrial intelligent life.

Extraterrestrial life is any form of life that exists outside of Earth. There is a lot of information that intelligent life from somewhere else in the universe came to Earth in the past and changed how people lived now.

Among the billions of planets in the universe, it seems possible that the conditions similar to those on Earth, where life has developed, could exist in many other places.

According to a commonly held theory, an *alien civilization* living on Earth before the emergence of our own influenced the evolution of Humans. Our planet would have been occupied by aliens long before the beginning of human civilization. They would have left traces and objects. Some may have even given their technological advancements to help our ancient civilizations.

Could humans live on another planet similar to Earth?

There are currently no travel plans. But scientists believe that the Milky Way is filled with habitable planets.

If the person next to me on a long airplane flight ever finds out that I am an astrophysicist, they would ask, with wide eyes, questions about life in the universe.

Experts from NASA and its partner institutions addressed this question at a public talk held at NASA Headquarters in Washington. They outlined NASA's roadmap to the search for life in the universe, an ongoing journey that involves a several current and future telescopes. Sara Seager predicts that in the near future, humans would be able to point out a star and say, *"That star has a planet like Earth* Sara Seager is a planetary science and physics professor at the Massachusetts Institute of Technology.

Astronomers think it is very likely that every single star in our Milky Way galaxy has at least one planet similar to ours.

Astronomers know there are planets out there that are similar to Earth in some ways and could have life on them. These *exoplanets* revolve around stars like our own sun but are far beyond our solar system.

Neil Alden Armstrong was the first man to set foot on the Moon on July 21, 1969, UTC, during the Apollo 11 mission. The most significant difference between *a trip to the Moon* and *a trip to distant planets* of our Galaxy lies in the distance that separates them from us. The technical challenges we face associated with such a trip are the ability to provide enough food and air to travellers. For now, it is the aspect of human survival in space that we understand least.

A life support system must provide astronauts quality air, water and food, etc., to travel 22 years at the speed of light before reaching a habitable planet.

A trip to another planet.

Compare Barbican's cannon-powered capsules of 1865 and 1870 to Neil Armstrong's moonwalk in 1969. During Apollo 11, could people travel to one of the 55 billion twin planets in our Galaxy?

Today's technology

Using NASA's Kepler Space Telescope, astronomers identified the first planet of Earth's size circling in the *habitable zone* of another star on April 17, 2014. The planet, "Kepler-186f" orbits an M dwarf, also known as a red dwarf, which comprise 70 percent of the stars in our galaxy, the Milky Way. The discovery of Kepler-186f verifies the existence of Earth-sized planets in the habitable zones of stars rather than our sun.

Kepler-186f is one of the five extra solar planets located around 490 light-years from Earth. The newly found exoplanets circles its sun at a distance of around 32.5 million miles (52.4 million kilometers). Kepler-186f takes about 130 days to orbit its red dwarf star.

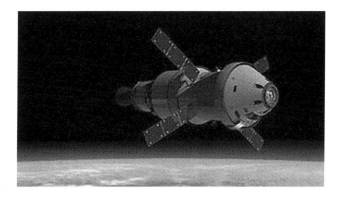

Space CEO Leon Musk introduced the Mars spacecraft, the spaceship his business plans to build to carry the first Mars colonists. The spaceship is designed to launch from Earth on top of the booster and travel the rest of its way to the Red Planet.

The plan is to send about 100 people per trip. Still, Musk hopes to eventually transport 200 or more passengers to reduce the cost per passenger. Depending on the year and technology, the journey may take as few as 80 days or as long as 150 days. The expected travel time will be reduced to 30 days *"in the more distant future."*

The rocket booster will have a diameter of 12 meters and the stack height will be 122 meters. The spaceship should hold a cargo of up to 450 tons depending on how many refills can be done with the tanker.

What Is Orion?

NASA's Orion spacecraft flew around Earth two times on a test flight. *This article is part of the **NASA Knows! (Grades K-4)** series. The* Orion spacecraft is a new NASA spacecraft. NASA intends for Orion to transport astronauts to an asteroid or even Mars.

What Will Orion Do?

When Orion takes the astronauts into space, it will launch on top of a huge rocket. NASA is building this rocket, the Space Launch System. This kind of rocket is called a heavy-lift launch vehicle. It will take Orion farther into space than people have been before.

Orion will use energy from the sun. Orion is equipped with solar panels that convert sunlight into power. The solar panels on the outside of the spaceship resemble the letter X. When Orion is in space, the solar panels will be powered by the sun.

Orion's First Flight

NASA wants to ensure that Orion performs its mission effectively and must operate securely. Hence, they must undergo testing before Orion or any other NASA spacecraft can launch.

Orion's maiden test flight was on December 5, 2014. The flight launched from Florida, Delta IV Heavy rocket carried Orion. Orion was tested without passengers. It orbited Earth twice. Four-and-a-half hours passed. The spaceship sped back to Earth; the spaceship landed near California.

Oct. 4, 2016

The Mars 2020 Lander Vision System was tested through NASA's Flight Opportunities Program.

An artist's concept of the 2012 Mars Curiosity Landing. Mars 2020 will use a nearly identical landing system with added precision from the Lander Vision System.

Credits: NASA Image /JPL-Caltech

NASA tested new "eyes" for its next Mars rover mission on a rocket built by Master Space Systems in Mojave, California, in 2014, thanks partly to NASA's Flight Opportunities Program, or FO program.

The agency's Jet Propulsion Laboratory in Pasadena, California, is leading the development of the Mars 2020 rover's Lander Vision System, or LVS. The prototype vision system launched 1,066 feet into the air aboard Marten's rocket-powered "Zombie" test platform. It guided the rocket to a precise landing at a predestinated target. LVS flew as part of a more extensive system of experimental landing technologies called the Autonomous Descent and Ascent Powered-flight Test bed, or ADAPT.

LVS, a camera-based navigation system, photographs the terrain beneath a descending spacecraft and matches it with onboard maps allowing the craft to detect its location relative to landing hazards such as boulders and outcroppings.

The system may then lead the drone toward a safe landing at its primary target or location or redirect it to the safer ground if there are dangers in the region. Imaging matching is aided by an inertial measurement unit that monitors orientation.

The Master flight tests under the Space Technology Mission Directorate were funded by the FO program. The program procures commercial suborbital space launch services to advance research, technology, and engineering related to NASA's space exploration mission. The program nurtures the emerging suborbital space industry while allowing NASA to concentrate on deep space.

The human space mission to Mars has been one of the long-term objectives in Astronautics since today. But the success of this project requires financial resources beyond those of the Apollo program. A Mars flight is a technical and human challenge not commensurate with a lunar expedition: the size of the vessels, closed circuit life support system over long periods (900 days), reliability of the equipment, psychological issues of a crew confined in a small space, physiological problems resulting from the absence of gravity on extended periods and the effect of radiation on the body.

A base on the Moon!

NASA embarked on an ambitious program to return man to the moon by installing a permanent base on the moon. Different from the adventure of Apollo, the Americans decided to settle a permanent headquarters on the Moon to prepare the first human mission to Mars.

Solar Energy is currently the sole feasible method for creating energy on the Moon, as no fossil fuels have yet been discovered on its surface. The moon base must be powered by photovoltaic panels. While technology has evolved and fears about the future of humanity on earth are progressing, the colonization of space could become a purpose possible and necessary. The moon would then be an excellent place for preparation in favour of more distant travel, to make a basis for the assembly of interplanetary ships.

The similarity between the Chariot of fire of God and our spacecraft interplanetary is astonishing.

I am perplexed about the Bible's legitimacy because of all the translations it has undergone over time.

The term of 'Bible' comes from the Greek word bibles, which means "books," according to the Old Testament and the New Testament (66 books total). At first, it was not a single book but a small series of books and pamphlets, separate books that were written on parchment rolls. The importance of the phases cannot be modified based on our views or perspectives, as is the case with all texts today.

The Christian tradition was much inspired by the character of Elijah, we can find his name everywhere in the New Testament. In the Gospel of Mark, the person of Elias is seen, as returning to earth before the coming of the Lord! John the Baptist and Elijah dress similarly (2 Kings 1.8 and Marc 1.6). Later in this Gospel, Jesus suggests that John the Baptist was Elijah who returned to Earth (Marc 9,13). The stories of the transfiguration of Jesus place Moses and Elijah in his company on the mount (Matthew 17: 1-9; Mark 9: 2-9 and Luke 9: 28-36). When people wonder who Jesus is, some say that it is Elijah who waited to announce the end of time.

What do they mean by chariot of fire at this time?

2 Kings 2:11King James Version (KJV)

> [11] *And it came to pass, as they still went on, and talked, that, behold, there appeared a chariot of fire, and horses of fire, and parted them both asunder; and Elijah went up by a whirlwind into heaven.*

2 Kings 6:17King James Version (KJV)

¹⁷ *And Elisha prayed, and said, Lord, I pray thee, open his eyes, that he may see. And the Lord opened the eyes of the young man; and he saw: and, behold, the mountain was full of horses and chariots of fire round about Elisha.*

Psalm 68:17King James Version (KJV)

¹⁷ *The chariots of God are twenty thousand, even thousands of angels: the Lord is among them, as in Sinai, in the holy place.*

1 Thessalonians 4:16-17King James Version (KJV)

¹⁶ *For the Lord himself shall descend from heaven with a shout, with the*

voice of the archangel, and with the trump of God: and the dead in Christ shall rise first.

[17] *Then we which are alive and remain shall be caught up together with them in the clouds, to meet the Lord in the air: and so, shall we ever be with the Lord.*

There is a description of the "Glory of God," which is the creator's flying machines. As you may have read on the departure of God's space ships, they are identical to ours today.

Talking of perfectly comparable takeoff and landings of our interplanetary flying machine, the primitive author of two thousand years ago speaks of horses of fire. If the people of more than 2,000 years ago witnessed the launch of our rockets today, they would return to their tribes while speaking of a fiery chariot drawn by spirited horses. They cannot rationally comprehend the scientific phenomenon and attribute it to supernatural mysticism and divine intervention.

The UFO

A recent Australian survey by *Readers Digest* showed that four out of five respondents believed that there is alien life in outer space. According to current statistics, 75 to 85 percent of the world's population believes in UFOs.

Being *God's ultimate creation*, the human race will advance to the point of constructing interplanetary spaceships that can go from Earth to one of the 55 billion planets that may have alien life or even an established society that can be found in our Galaxy. This evolution might involve the ability to create new worlds like ours or rehabilitate abandoned planets from disasters or wars.

Genesis 1:26-27: *"God created man in his own image, likeness, man and woman."*

Psalms 82
82.6 I said: you are gods; you are all sons of the highest.

John 10:34-35
[34] *Jesus answered them: is it not written in your law: I said: you are gods?*

In the Catholic Church, the Jews, like many Christian pastors, when questioned on this subject, refuse the actual definition of Genesis 1:26-27 (*in his image*) and always turn to the second part of the verse (*likeness*) because its intention is less explicit. None of them can read these verses without withdrawing or adding words to change the definition, none accept the legal description of *"God created man in his own image."*

What do Mormons believe?

The name *Mormon,* which members of the Church of Jesus Christ of Latter-day Saints don't mind being called, comes from the book of Mormon. This church teaches that God, our Heavenly Father, and our creator; was born of a father and a mother like I was. He lived and died in a place like ours, somewhere in the universe. He has now moved on to a higher place.

The guest delivered a speech to an assembly of around 20,000 Church members at a general conference conducted shortly after the death of one of his friends, King Follet. King Follett

Sermon, one of the classics of Church literature, was given by the Prophet Joseph Smith at April 7, 1844, conference of the Church in Nauvoo, Illinois. There were about 20,000 saints there. In the description of the talk, it was said that it was the funeral sermon for Elder King Follet, a close friend of the Prophet's who had died in an accident on March 9.

Part of his sermon (God an Exalted Man)

I will go back to the beginning before the world was, to show what kind of a being God is. What sort of a being was God in the beginning? Open your ears and hear, all ye ends of the earth, for I am going to prove it to you by the Bible, and to tell you the designs of God in relation to the human race, and why He interferes with the affairs of man.

God was once similar to us, a holy man, and sits enthroned in yonder heavens! That is the great secret. If the veil was opened today, and the Great

God who holds this world in its orbit, who upholds all worlds and all things by His power, were to make himself visible—I say you would see him like a man in form—like yourselves in image, and very similar as a man; like how Adam was created in the very similar fashion, image and likeness of God. Adam also received instruction from, walked, talked and conversed with Him, like how two people usually talk to each other.

I'll tell you how God became God so that you can understand the subject of the dead and give comfort to those who are weeping their friends. We thought that God was eternal. I'll disprove it and remove the veil so that you may see.

Some may find these basic notions incomprehensible. The first principle of the gospel is that we must know for sure what God is like so that we can talk to Him like we talk to other people, and that He was once a man like us. Yes, God, the

Father of all of us, lived on Earth, just like Jesus Christ did, and I will show you this from the Bible.

As Jules Verne imagined walking on the Moon, let's assume what may happen to some of us in the future. Assuming that the space technology continues to advance at its current rate, let us imagine for a moment that instead of 1865 and 1870, the writing took place in 2016. He described his journey not travelling around the Moon but he used the new *NASA Spacecraft Orion*, which has been improved and can now carry astronauts in our galaxy and beyond. It can even travel Kepler-186f; one of the five planets found on the different solar systems located about 490 light-years from Earth.

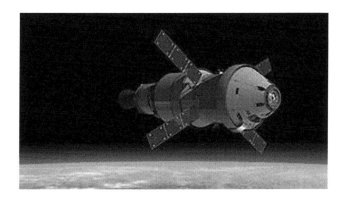

Imagine that the newly improved NASA Spacecraft Orion now travelling at ten light-years an hrs with one hundred people aboard, a fifty hrs journey one way to Kepler-186f one of the remarkable planets of our galaxy.

Vegetal and animal lives proliferate everywhere, on the surface like in the water, an earthly paradise, the Garden of Eden on Earth! The existence of human was the only thing lacking.

The hundred people setting foot on Kepler-186f felt like Adam and Eve in the garden in Eden, as reported in Genesis 1:27-28 (King James

Version). They only had to be fruitful, multiply themselves to fill Kepler-186f and subdue it, have dominion over the fish of the sea, the flow of the air, and every living thing that moved upon Kepler-186f. They had to increase and develop their population up to fullness.

Like us, they will go to another beautiful planet after thousands of years or even beyond the universe to start a new world, and/or simply visit other humans existing.

CONCLUSION

Religions have taught us of irrational doctrines opposite to the Bible and its teaching standards. Even today, their theories remain firm in our thoughts, despite our efforts to remove them. Since Constantine (307-337 A.D. up to the 1940s), the Catholic and other faiths have propagated myths and tales from generation to generation and are currently attempting to regenerate in various ways.

Neither the egg nor the chicken, or the rooster came first. There has never been a first among the three, because anyone of the three needed the two others to exist. Yes, there was in the past, and there will be in the future, a new beginning, the birth of an animal, human, planetary systems or extraterrestrial creations. Still, it always is the result of a succession of the combination of seeds or embryos.

Everything in the whole world, minerals, animals, etc., is made to perpetuate itself, and extend its offspring eternally; it is an endless transformation. Everything that lives and dies simply transforms, leading to a new and authentic life.

There is no doubt in my perspective that Earth-dwelling humans exist on some of the billion planets comparable to our own in our galaxy and the vastness of the cosmos, and that, with a little adaption, they will maintain our species forever!

Big Bang is a cosmological model used by some scientists to describe the origin and evolution of the universe, which is not funded.

According to the proponents of the Big Bang, the universe exploded 13.7 billion years ago due to a small point that existed during intense heat and density. If the universe was not created 13.7 billion years ago, how could it have been hot? If the galaxies were moving away at a more incredible speed than they are distant, imagine the distance and the speed they would now have reached between them after 13.7 billion years at that ratio.

To believe that God created the heavens and the Earth from nothing, we must add it ourselves; *the Bible never mentions it.*

No matter when He created the universe, the time between having always existed and the date He created the world is innumerable, and beyond description. The theory of a God who existed eternally but not the universe seems very unconvincing to me.

When they preached the dialogue of religions, there was instead the *revival of the war of religions.* All the time, religion was and still the most important cause for wars. From Martin Luther to Bin Laden, millions and millions of people died for God.

The perception of religious faith is similar regardless if they are Muslim, Christian, Jewish or Buddhist; defaming a religion inevitably hurts its faithful members. Karl Marx, philosopher and historian, was entirely accurate declaring that *"religion is the opium of the people."* Many world leaders understood the religion's importance in motivating people to give their lives to reach their goals. Saddam Hussein, appealed to God repeatedly against an *"evil enemy."*

Albert Einstein received the *Nobel Prize for Physics* in 1921 for his explanation of the *photoelectric effect.* He is today considered as one of the greatest scientists in history, and his fame reached far beyond the scientific community. The *Theory of Relativity* was developed by Albert Einstein in the early 20th century.

Albert Einstein's initial idea was that *the universe is static, does not evolve with time, so stable and eternal* so obviously contradicts the doctrine of creation by the Catholic Church and some of our scientists. Additionally, Georges Lemaître, backed by his observational evidence, concluded that our universe was expanding in 1927. Einstein rejected Friedman's as well as Lemaitre's findings.

The Big Bang Theory is based on the work of Monsignor Georges Lemaitre, a Belgian Catholic Canon, astronomer and physicist, who used his *"Primitive Atom Theory"* to explain the creation of the universe.

Monsignor Georges Lemaitre, and all the religious power leading the education and a large part of the governments in the world, made sure that Albert Einstein's theory, contradicting the creation preached by the Catholic Religion, is vanished from the shelf of our institutions.

Extraterrestrial life is any form of life that exists outside of Earth. If this is the case, we could say that when Apollo 11, the first man mission with a crew of three astronauts, became Aliens from the Earth on the surface of the moon, they turn out to be the first extra Lunar known today.

Being God's ultimate creation, the human race will advance to the point of constructing interplanetary spaceships that can go from Earth to one of the 55 billion planets that may have alien life or even an established society that can be found in our Galaxy. This evolution might involve the ability to create new worlds like ours or rehabilitate abandoned planets from disasters or wars.

Real Courchesne

Made in the USA
Columbia, SC
19 October 2022

69739768R00050